MW00328090

her favorite color was
sunshine yellow

Copyright © 2020 by Amanda Karch

All rights reserved. No part of this book may be used or reproduced in any manner without written permission except in the case of reprints or brief quotations in the context of reviews.

www.akkwriting.com
IG: @akkwriting

Paperback ISBN: 978-1-7359639-0-7
E-book ISBN: 978-1-7359639-1-4

Cover art by Sri K. (IG: @poetrybysri)

her favorite color was
sunshine yellow

amanda karch

for Ethan -
my inspiration and my love

my words are tied in knots,
strings of my life forever
tangled,
twisted and tongue-tied
by you

I try
to get the right ones across,
untangling as I go
but
I'll never be able to describe
what lives in my heart for you

but I will spend my life trying

the color of lonely is not gray
or black or blue.
it has no color
because you can see
straight through my tears and know
the root of them is
missing you.

I'm watching the shadows dance across the wall
and wishing they were us.
back when life was simple,
back when a touch was a possibility
and not just a wistful dream,
back when I could be so happy
with you by my side,
when you could take my hand and
twirl me around in a circle.
me: drunk on life, love, and you.
endlessly spinning,
dizzy from
fa
  ll
    ing
      in love with you
      all over again like it was the first day.

my reality is better than my dreams but
I know my dreams are the path to a future
where I no longer sleep lonely

the feeling of
looking at a word and
knowing it's spelled right but
it doesn't look right
or,
the feeling of looking at the
empty space in my bed where you should be

and I know you can't, but I want you here

waiting,
staring at the cracks in the ceiling,
tracing their path with eyes that
only want to see you,
wishing the world could open, swallow me up
only to put me right next to you.
it's a sad world when you're not in it with me.

an hour and then some:
that's all that separates us but it may as well be
an ocean that I can't swim across.
and I try.
if I can't physically, I try to feel like I'm with you
in spirit -

> hugging my pillow close like it's my arms
> wrapped around you, head on your chest;
> cuddled up in your sweatshirt, wishing it
> were you; sending you kisses through the
> phone but oh so desperately wanting the
> feeling of your lips on mine.

I'm just waiting, love,

until I can get to you again

salty tears
or,
a rainfall on cheeks

you can pick, but the feeling is the same

it's Sunday
but I have the lazy day blues -
for these are our mornings
of lounging, laughing and
a whole lot of loving
but I can't do it alone.

Sundays just aren't the same
without you
and your body pressed against mine,
me into we and
never separating.

don't let me go.

even if it is just a morning daydream

lingering
      shadows of light on my skin:
ghosts
      of your touch

and so we wait.
on opposite shores,
seemingly an ocean apart
but able to see across the waves.

but we're under the same stars,

and they shine so bright,
at their most when the lights are dimmed
like the mood that creeps up when we're apart for
so long,
but they shine,
a beacon of hope in a fog of loneliness,
so I know our love shines too.

but we're under the same moon,

and its shape waxes and wanes with the tides,
but I watch the waves between us,
and just as they ebb out,
they flow back in,
so I know that no matter where our love takes us,
it will hold its strength and shape.

and so we wait.
and we will.
because it's not just for one time together -

we're waiting for our forever

I have
sunset stains on my fingertips
from reaching out to touch the sky
because it's made of the same hues you see and
maybe
just maybe
I can feel you through the
late summer sunshine
beaming across your face,

my favorite smile

don't be afraid to be the one who loves the most

ebbing and flowing with the tide.

not the feeling:
no.
the feelings are rooted into the sandy bottom of
the sea,
jetty rocks,
toes buried in sand
chasing hermit crabs.

it's the moments of happiness,
riding the waves as they come
crashing to shore,
and the moments of saltwater tears
that play a game of tag,
you're it,
with distance as its silent player.

love is hard.

especially when the number of miles you are apart
from each other seems infinite and there is no
road to get between;

especially when darkness falls and all you want is
the whisper of his voice in your ear, telling you he
loves you, pulling you close before you d r i f t off
into a dreamless sleep -

because how can they happen when you're living
in one?

but love is beautiful.

especially when hearing his voice, seeing his name,
reading his words draw the smile right onto your
face with a marker so permanent that nothing
could ever erase it;

especially when the sun rises and you're the first
thing on his mind, and he on yours, and life just
seems so right when you are both daydreaming of
the good days to come when you are both free.

you swept me off my feet
but
as much as I love dancing,
I don't need a ball -
I just want to know:

when do we get our fairytale ending?

midnight tolls the clock
inside my heart,
knowing it's another day past
when I need you
but still the hour of feeling
the phantom space beside me
where you belong

I woke up like
salt in a wound,
tears streaming down my face like
whitewater rapids I don't want to experience,
heart racing,
catching in my throat like a stop sign that
appeared out of nowhere,

immediately rolling over and wanting to
hug you close to me,
make sure you really were there and
safe and
here for me,

why aren't you here?

time doesn't like to stand still
for us -
forever
a game of cat and mouse,
hide and seek,
wishing it would lose its breath so time could

freeze.

and we could enjoy our forever
now.

without you,
like a broken compass needle
spinning erratically,
I am lost
til your touch centers me and
I can find my way home
with you

don't let me sleep lonely

someday,
I know the only commute I'll have to you is to
the other side of the bed

the night sky smiles when it sees us together
but when you're not here,
I stare up at the stars
counting each one.
but I only count to one each time.
because then
every star is the first star I see,
and that means
more times I get to wish
for you to be by my side.

is there some place where
tears don't grow on trees?
because
I miss you but
my heart is still beating
and breathing the same air as you,
a few hundred miles removed,
but
if I try hard enough,
I can feel the ghost of
your lips touching mine.

trying to capture your scent from this t-shirt is like
trying to hold hands with the wind

five o'clock shadow
of your lips on mine,

half past *I want you,*
quarter to *I miss you,*

remembering how it felt
with the collar of your shirt
tightly wrapped in my fist,
aching with desire,
begging with that look in my eyes -

those lips on mine:
not *I want you* but
I need you kisses

the endless tease of being away from you

whispers across cell phone towers
and visits cut too short by nightfall
can only do so much
when
miles away lies my heart,
home where it belongs with you

old photographs like cinnamon,
                    sugar-sweet with nostalgia

things that make me wonder:

1. tears
why do they never end? I know some infinities
are bigger than others, but that means some are
smaller, so why can't you come home and help me
dry them? because my eyes are flooding and my
insurance policy is you.

2. empty beds
why are they so cold? I know we still have our
spark, so shouldn't that warm me? or is distance
the sand that smothers the fire and leaves me
lonely in the dark?

3. sunsets
why aren't the colors as bright? did you take the
sky's paintbrushes with you when I gave you a
piece of my heart for safekeeping when you had
to leave? those colors reminded me of you, love,
but I want more than painted skies.

I want you back

is there a language where
goodbye means *I'm coming home*
or
I miss you means *I'll see you soon?*

because I'm wishing that
my translations were wrong,
meaning lost across distance,

though I'm no interpreter,
and I know three little words always hold true

they say
if you love something,
let it go

which is why I am so calm in letting my
sun set,
sighing with nothing but contentment,
warmed by awe
despite my frozen hands,

colors melting together
as they get closer to shore
and I'm sure
they were put there for us

because they say
if you love something,
let it go
and if it's meant to be,
it will come back to you

and just as I know
the sun will set over the water again,

I know
days like this with you are
meant to be

and the colors of today are forever in my heart

being the romantic that I am,
gazing out of my window and
seeing those
purples and pinks and oranges and yellows
all strewn across the sky,
painted on my favorite canvas,
calming the earth one stripe at a time,

I thought

tonight is the night
I should be seeing you again.

it just seemed right.

my favorite person
with me under my favorite sky.

nothing seemed more perfect,
more right.

and somehow I knew

distance is
shaded in both sunshine yellow and shadow gray,
yin and yang,
but lined with silver
that pulls us closer -
magnetism
never letting us be apart for long

I was dreaming of you my whole life.

                        I never knew it, but it was you.

I dreamed of smiles that hurt to let go,
hugs that welded two bodies into one,
kisses that tasted of sunshine and salty air,
a vacation that was never-ending.
you were the ocean

                        and I was the sand.

two bodies endlessly interwoven
       but always dancing out of reach for a time.
never a fault of our own -
the tides were what kept us from always being
layered together,
top,
bottom,
everything in between.
time and circumstance were the tides,
pulsing,
while our love was fighting against the current.
but even as we're swimming,
we will never drown.
your waves will catch me,
bring me to shore,

             and I will give us a place to stand,
             toes buried in the sand because I am
                   never letting go.

not when our love tastes like salt and
burns like sunshine yellow.
and we can watch the sun set
over the waters together,
but we both know it will rise again in the morning,
when I am waking up next to you.

and to think

one night I walked out alone,
drunk and giddy,
seeing signs in the words we shared,
but just as I thought there were the
beginnings of a spark,
you put out the fire and we went
our separate ways

but

two nights later, I was
grabbing you by the hand and
                    (an hour passing) you were
grabbing me by the hips and
                    (minutes passing) we were
lips locked,
against the wall in our own little world

and to think

all was right in the world
from that moment on

he was hello from his first goodbye,
the type of smile you never wanted to lose.

he was the breath of fresh air in a crowded space,
creating a safe haven that made you feel like
you were the only two people in the world that
mattered.

and it's true.

all that matters is us,
me and you,
you and I,

causing goodbyes to paint a shade of gray over
the colorful life we live,
but the hellos make life worth living,
sneaking through the clouds as a rainbow

except that happiness never disappears

you pick flowers for me
except the petals are
ink-dyed
and the stem is
honesty
and they are words
tied in bouquets just for me

but they smell even sweeter

if I asked you for a night of stargazing,
you'd lasso the stars and give them to me,
sparkling just like your eyes
when you smile -
the dream I never want to end
                    because sleeping next to you is
                            all I could ever want,
                        but waking up next to you is
                            all I could ever need.

if I asked you to watch the sunset with me,
you'd paint the sky yourself so it would be
beautiful -
the sun slipping away for one more night,
but our hearts are here to stay,
                        beating in unison to your
                        colors dancing across the
                            canvas of a sky,
                        but my heart skips a beat
                    whenever my eyes meet yours.

you'd give me the world, but I'll give you my heart

blue meeting green,
two colors on the same side of the wheel but
with different souls that
converge with a single glance saying
all we need to know.

our eyes say it all

maybe our colors bled together
or
we got them mixed up
but together we traced
daydreams on each other's skin -
kisses, our only paintbrush.

we may have never painted by the numbers
but I'd never trade what we have.

you make me smile
always,
in all ways:

my eyes light up with a sparkle
that's been missing since I believed in
imaginary friends and pixie dust,

my skin smirks,
shivering with even the slightest touch,
a whisper of promises to come,

but most of all,
my heart is beaming,
outshining even the sun,
for your words are enough to guide me
through any nightfall.

sunlight kissing your eyes,
breaking night's shadow
as your lips meet mine

your kisses are like:

butterflies' wings,
a feather tickling the back of your neck
with every breath,
fresh air,
the waves knocking you off your feet
time and time again,
an endless yearning for more,
forever.

it's you,
it's only you,

and if it's not, I don't know why the universe
would tease me like this.

and you know I like to be teased,

but that's by the soft graze of
your fingertips over the parts
of my skin that send pulses of
electricity throughout my body,
lighting me up with sparks that
fly and catch when they reach you.

and then we're both burning together
but it's a heat we both want,
fusing us together as one,
all the way down to the
very edges of our
souls.

one arm under my shirt,
above my heart -
where it belongs.
a piece of you with a piece of me
which is only fitting
                    since you make me feel complete.

legs tangled under sheets
and you can't tell where one of us ends and
another begins,
joined at the hips -
a joke but true,
                because I never want to leave your side.

side by side.
your face looking at the back of my head
but you don't have to see
    my eyes to know they're closed in contentment,
        my lips to know they're upturned in a smile,
            my heart to know it's fully open for you.

before we drift

dreaming,
wishing upon a star and
another and another,
til my mind is filled with starlight and
goodnight kisses and
secret smiles and glances that only I understand,
yearning for this to be forever,
not understanding how it could be
anything but

a lifetime spent with you

it's so easy to string words together like
seashells on a necklace but
keeping them is the hard part.

but I know someday you will
clasp that necklace around my neck,
finger trailing right past your favorite spot to kiss,
lips brushing against my ear to whisper:

"we kept our promise."

you asked me
if I'd live somewhere warm with you

but I already live hand-in-hand with the type of
happiness that fills you with warmth, bubbling up
uncontrollably because it's endless,

it's you

golden hour:
sunlight kissing the earth
or,
every hour your smile reflects the
lightness in your heart

you're a summer breeze:
refreshing yet calming,
soothing my skin and my soul,
whispering into my ear a secret meant just for me
but whisked away when the rays of
sunshine yellow caress my face,
but hidden in the warmth is another whisper,
one that says:

forever and always

I see sunsets in your eyes,
a reflection of the good memories,

        but sunrises in your heart,
     a sign of the memories to come

while most people turn my poetry into
fragmented paragraphs
run-on sentences
broken words

you weave it into
music
and the wind sings to me
and we slow dance
to the words that no one hears aloud
but can be found on repeat
in our hearts

it's twirling me around a candy store but the
sweetest thing is the smile on your face

no matter how hard the rain,
your smile is

sunshine incarnate

things I left behind
(since meeting you):

self-conscious thoughts,
cold winter nights,
lonely hands holding themselves,
a wandering, overthinking mind,
searching for answers why,
storebought pajamas *(because now it's only your shirts)*,
relying on words as my only solace,
fear of the unknown,
a grayscale world

because you fill my world with color

I never liked nicknames
til mine crossed your lips
like sugar

my name
on your lips,
just a whisper
but it knocks loudly on my heart,
tumbling down doors
to which it holds the only key.

so simple,
this one word pillow talk,
but it's all I need to

come undone

you and me,
we make perfect poetry
sneaking kisses under trees
and dreaming of more *our's* and *we's*

for the longest time I've been trying to say it
without saying it
but your smile runs through my veins and
I can't hide it anymore.

you're my lifeline:
the one I can always count on to
tease that smile onto my face
and make sure it sticks,
drawing it on with
permanent marker because you know
just how to get to me because
you're my one and only,
my one true smile that can multiply into a million
and even into infinity
because that's what I feel for you -
infinite amounts of that feeling
of sunshine yellow and
pure pure happiness.

you can ask, but you already know the answer

you told me I was the
culmination of all the prettiest sunsets
and that was the day I finally saw
what you see in me

the only way I can describe it is indescribable.
you can't measure the amount of love I have for
you because it overflows out of me with every
extra smile you cause and every extra laugh you
make because
you're mine.
and it amazes me sometimes, how I got to be so
lucky to be with someone who makes me feel like
sunshine yellow, no matter the color of the day
because
everything is black and white compared to you.
you brighten my life in an unimaginable way that
is so very real but makes me feel like I am in a
constant state of dreaming but every time I wake
up it's next to you so I know that
what we have is real.
and true.
and deep.
so true that every word you say to me is forever a
gift and I never forget the present.
so deep that I never want to escape but who wants
to escape a reality that feels like a fantasy?
all I know is that you would make nonsense make
sense for me,
that you would do anything to make me feel
sunshine yellow even on the darkest day,
and that I will never stop loving you.

indescribably, madly in love with my best friend

two tenses:
present and future.
the only thing that matters is the
what is
and the
what will be.

its preposition is
with
and its pronoun is
ours

for it's my life *with* yours that makes it
ours.

so kiss me with every word you can,
it doesn't need a translation

I'm fluent in our language of love

it's a laying under the stars at 2am kind of love,
or a chasing sunsets across the waves kind of love,
a talking about your deepest secrets and fears
but not a wishing on a star kind of love,

because we both know it's a future kind of love

curious,
isn't it,
how someone can capture your soul,
wild love, flaws and all
and make it their own
where everything they touch turns to gold
and finally you feel
valued,
appreciated,
loved
like you are the star their planet orbits

but they are your universe

the stars speak to me when I'm with you.

I remember
reclining in car seats,
necks craned back to see the sky
through smudged glass,
all that was separating us
between fields of open air.

I remember
searching for shooting stars,
anxious for one to wish on,
so I could hold onto this moment

                        forever.

and I remember
they told me

            this was going to be my always

waking up to arms pressed tightly around me
as my body moves to fit right against yours,
two puzzle pieces finding their match,
half-asleep but still
reaching for your hand to know that
you're there for me
always,
your head nuzzling into my neck,
feeling the tickle of your breath on my skin,
drifting,
       drifting away
into a dreamland that never fades,
even when our eyes both open,
your lips twitching into a smile
that I feel on my skin
as I turn to face it -
           my favorite smile,
eyes still half-closed,
mind still half-asleep,
but I still manage to find your lips with mine,
that smile of yours brushing lightly across a
growing one of my own,
knowing even in the morning fog that clouds my
mind,
you're the ray of sunshine that always gets through,
starting my morning just how I want every day to be:
together
     in love
        with you.

my Sunday kinda love

no more stars in the sky but
still wishing for this morning
always.

love me til I'm both
overwhelmed in my senses and
kissed senseless by you

the sparks
       igniting my skin under your touch.
the sheen
       of our bodies as we leave
       no room for oxygen.

but I'm
       surviving on you
              in this heat wave.

when you look out over the ocean,
you can see the heat rising above the waves,
a shimmer in the air like
                              electricity
or,

your hands
tracing delicate lines
down
        my
              thigh

and there you are:
laughing at my goosebumps,
despite this hot summer sun

I wish
I could bottle up
this feeling,
because it's so much more than
sunshine yellow.

it's
dragonflies,
       where I found the one that's the most rare,
       because who else has a love this special?

it's
wide open fields
       filled with endless possibility,
       green with the taste of
       sunscreen-kissed skin that
       lingers on your lips.

but, most of all, it's
you:
       a whirlwind of
       breathlessness,
       green eyes,
       tight hugs and
       forever,
          endless
             love.

your morning smile
like dew on grass from last night's rain,
breathing life into my world

I just want to love you

and you know I do because
it's ingrained within me,
a part of my DNA,
my soul,
so I know it's true

but there are some days where
I just need to love you,
hold you close,
wrap my arms around you and
hear our hearts beat in sync,

and whisper to you a thousand and one times that
I love you,
but it still won't be enough to get my point across,
because how can so much meaning fit into
three
    little
        words?

and I know you know,
but sometimes I just need to say it again because
I'm pulled to you like gravity and
I'm dragged deeper into our love every day.

so let me hold you,
and we can fall together,
because falling in love is the best type of falling.

and I'm still falling for you more every day

I love you

                            you love me more

I love you most -

you always let me win it.

a shadow trying to steal my
sunshine yellow
might say:

It's because you love him more

but

you tell me
you love me forever

                    and how can you beat that?

            I call it a tie, but together we're winning

hand-in-hand swinging
like playground innocence,
loving purely

they say some infinities are bigger than others
and some loves are bigger than other loves,
but our love knows no limits
because every day it grows.

just as the sun rises,
the sun sets every day,
and I am just as sure that
our love grows with
every ray of sunshine yellow
you bring into my life.

if a miracle dissolved on my tongue,
I'd wish to taste
the salt on our skin
after wading out til the depths couldn't match
how deeply my happiness is entwined
in yours because
aren't miracles just synonyms for the unexplained?
and
although I will never stop telling you
how much I love you,
no amount of words,
sunshine-kissed or not,
can explain it fully.

all I wanted was a reminder of
the perfect memory,
and the bracelet was the closest thing I could find to
say:

you are my best friend and
I never want to leave you and
missing you is hell but being with you is heaven and
I appreciate you and
I need you and
I love you,
but "joy" was the closest I could choose.
and it was heads up, printed on a penny,
tied around my wrist with the message in my heart,
so I wished
but won't tell

because I want it to come true

wonderland:

a broad definition contains
my dreams of you and I,
wrapped in a ribbon of
love, passion, and bliss
and I never want to be awoken because

asleep in your arms is
where I should always be at the end of the day.

lovers' waltz:

your hands.

my lips.

harmony.

they say if you like someone,
you'll lean toward them,
a natural tilt
finding your way inside of their bubble.

then, love,
I'm crooked
and I never want to be anything else:
falling
        over from leaning so close because I'm
falling
        in love with you more every day.

save some space for me -
not much
        because you know how I like to cuddle up
but leave room for our future

        because I know I have found it with you

I'm sorry
     I always steal the blanket

but maybe

I'm just hoping it will make you
hold me
     a little closer
because

I'll always keep your heart warm

your lips caress my name
like pillows

never wake me up from this dream

fire-kissed skies are
what my dreams are made of,
love burning an eternal flame in my heart,
your soft kisses on my nose to make me
laugh your favorite laugh,
and open skies showing us there's
no limit to where life will take us

take my hand.

pull me alongside you
up mountains,
across beaches,
through shadowed forest trails and
city streets.
as long as you keep holding on,
I'll never let go -
                    I'm stuck to you like
                    the moon in the sky:
                    a permanent fixture

        as this adventure unfolds between us

a series of instants is all it took.

a hand.
grabbing another, pulling it into a space where
there was no space, yet somehow enough for two.

a dance.
what started off so innocent that slowly turned
into two bodies closing the gap between them,
finding infinite space in a crowded room where
the focus was only on each other.

a question.
mistaken and laughed off at first, but repeated.
meaning understood, the beginning of a night
written in the stars. hands. on hips. space closing
until one body begins where another ends.

a kiss.
and another. one melting into the next while voices
blur on all sides but the only one that matters is the
one whispering in my ear, the one taking my hand
(a hint of what's to come) and leading me past
the throngs of people who will talk about it in the
morning but they don't matter.

because the stars are out,
lighting a path that shows our future even though
we both might not know it yet,
a new home because it's where my heart is.

> *and I know now, even if I didn't then,*
> *my heart is infinitely with you*

in a sea of people, of worries, of cares,
he was the wave that swept me off of my feet.
I fell hard
but falling was the best thing for me because
I fell in love
with a man who traced patterns on my skin,
with his hands and with his lips,
that had a language of their own, but
I knew they all translated to
I love you.
because he did
and he does
and there's no cloud of doubt to fog my mind
because his smile is the ray of
sunshine yellow that cuts through any darkness.
the color that encapsulates
the feeling that encompasses me
when he tucks a strand of hair behind my ear
for a kiss,

or when his laughs echo mine with a smile that
makes my heart skip a beat,
or when I catch him staring at me with
that look in his eyes, the one that says
you're mine, forever, now, and always.
and I want *always* to be synonymous to *us,*
two words that can be used interchangeably but
we can't be changed because
why would you ever want to change
what makes you happy?

so then it's just us.

letting the tide take us wherever the future holds,
drifting away on a dream,
hands interlocked,
holding fast under sunset-painted skies,
simply waiting for the sun to rise on the day
where we know it's
always us
and
us always.

the future we both want

he writes poems for me:
a piece of my heart
giving me
a piece of my soul.

but what he doesn't understand is that,
to me,

he is my poetry

I'm not sure if soulmates exist

but if they do,
I want mine to be you.
I mean someone who is
sharing a part of my soul.
you,
      intertwining yours,
                with mine.
no boundaries marking where we separate,
because our love knows no bounds
and as we grow and change every day,
our soul changes,
            grows with us,
a different form, a different shape but
the same love within
because

why would you want to give up a part of yourself?

her favorite color was never yellow:
always the oranges from the sunset skies,
brush strokes weaving in and out of the clouds,

or the grays that enveloped her room,
soothing,
calming,
showing her the world was not always
black and white,
but painted in shades between.

her favorite color was never yellow:
it was either too pastel -

                child's play that did not match
                the sophistication of her mind

or too bold -

                and she never liked being
                the center of attention anyway.

her favorite color was never yellow,
but then he came into her life
in a whirlwind of soft smiles,
teasing fingertips,
strong arms that only wanted to hold her close
and never let go,

and he brought with him the sunlight that trailed
behind, the opposite of a shadow,
for he only brightened the room when he entered.

and so then,
her favorite color was sunshine yellow.
and she never knew how she thought otherwise.

For more poetry, writing, and content by
Amanda Karch, follow her on Instagram
@akkwriting or visit her website at
www.akkwriting.com.

Made in the USA
Middletown, DE
14 January 2021

31645725R00066